Money

Mindset

Makeover:

Transform Your Beliefs to
Attract Abundance

Copyright Contents

Table of Contents

Chapter 1: The Power of Your Money Mindset

Welcome to the life-changing experience that is "Money Mindset Makeover: Transform Your Beliefs to Attract Abundance." In this first part, we'll look into the interesting and sometimes overlooked area of money thinking. We'll look at why your money attitude is more than simply a passing notion and how it affects your financial performance. By the conclusion of this chapter, you will have a better knowledge of how your money beliefs and attitudes affect your financial well-being and how a money mentality makeover is your key to attracting wealth into your life.

The Financial Mindset Evolution

Whether we like it or not, money is an important element of our lives. It is the mechanism by which we get our fundamental needs, pursue our desires, and attain our objectives. Despite its evident significance, many individuals fail to investigate their connection with money. This error may have serious ramifications for one's financial performance and general well-being.

As the cornerstone of your financial journey, your money mentality is the collection of ideas, attitudes, and assumptions you have about money. These ideas are firmly embedded in your brain and impact how you make financial choices, establish goals, and see possibilities. Your money mentality is the prism through which you see the world of finances, and it has a huge impact on the outcomes you obtain.

The Mind-Body Relationship

Consider your money attitude to be the link that connects your ideas to your financial realities. A healthy money attitude may improve your financial well-being in the same way that a good mindset can improve your physical health. Indeed, recent research in psychology and behavioral economics has shown a strong link between your ideas and your financial performance.

Consider the following scenario: You're given a new employment opportunity that comes with a bigger income but also more responsibilities. If your money perspective is based on fear and scarcity, you may find yourself hesitant to accept greater financial responsibilities. If, on the other hand, you have a growth-oriented money attitude, you will likely view this as an opportunity for personal and financial progress, joyfully grasping the possibility of better wages and improved financial security.

The Subconscious Effect

One of the most fascinating elements of the money mentality is that it operates mostly subconsciously. Most of our everyday financial choices, from saving to spending, are impacted by ideas we may or may not be aware of. These ingrained views are often influenced by our upbringing, societal influences, and prior experiences.

For example, if you grew up in a home where money was usually a cause of stress or concern, you may have formed a scarcity money mentality, thinking that money is always limited and financial success is out of reach. This irrational assumption may lead to self-destructive actions such as overspending or under-earning, perpetuating the scarcity cycle.

Prophecies That Fulfill Themselves

The money mindset's potency stems from its self-fulfilling nature. If you convince yourself that you'll never be rich, your behaviors will reflect that idea. You may pass up financial possibilities or undermine your attempts to enhance your financial status. Someone who has a positive money attitude and believes in their abilities to produce wealth, on the other hand, is more inclined to take controlled risks and seek financial chances with confidence.

Let us put this notion into context with an example. Consider two people with comparable talents and credentials who have the chance to establish their enterprises. One has an abundant attitude when it comes to money, feeling that financial success is within their grasp. The other has a scarcity mentality when it comes to money, fearing financial failure. In this case, the individual with an abundant mentality is more likely to take risks, put in the required work, and persevere in the face of obstacles, improving their chances of success. The scarcity mentality, on the other hand, may not even try to establish a company because they believe it would fail.

The Importance of Perception

Your financial attitude influences your perspective of possibilities and obstacles. Challenges are seen as chances for learning and progress by someone with a growth-oriented money perspective. They are more willing to take measured chances, adapt to change, and see failures as temporary setbacks. A scarcity mentality, on the other hand, may regard hurdles as insurmountable impediments, leading to avoidance or giving up when confronted with difficulties.

Take, for example, the notion of stock market investment. A person with an abundant mentality may view it as a chance to expand their money and be willing to learn about the stock market. They will most likely approach it with excitement and a desire to learn about the complexities of investment. A person with a scarcity mentality, on the other hand, may perceive the stock market as excessively hazardous and confusing, deciding to shun it entirely, losing out on the potential rewards of long-term investment.

Your Financial Mindset: A Self-Portrait

To genuinely alter your financial life, you must first identify and comprehend your existing money perspective. Your money mentality is a reflection of your ideas, beliefs, and experiences. To enhance this self-portrait, take a step back and look at it critically. Only then will you be able to start making the required modifications and creating a new masterpiece?

This self-portrait may reflect a range of characteristics, such as:

Do you feel there is enough money to go around, or do you perceive it as a limited resource that others are hogging?

Growth vs. Fixed: Do you feel your money can expand over time, or do you believe your financial condition is fixed and unchangeable?

Optimism vs. Pessimism: Do you tend to be positive about your financial prospects, or do you regularly foresee financial difficulties?

Fear vs. bravery: Do you face financial difficulties and possibilities with bravery, or do you shy away from them out of fear?

How do you deal with financial setbacks? Are you resilient or helpless? Do you feel resilient and motivated to recover, or do you feel powerless and defeated?

Understanding where you stand on these attributes gives you insight into your money mentality, helping you to make educated choices about the ideas and attitudes you want to alter.

The Road Ahead

Keep in mind that your financial success is not only driven by external variables such as income, investments, or economic situations as we continue on our path to shift your money perspective. Your inner world—your ideas, attitudes, and thoughts—plays a critical part in determining your financial reality.

We'll look at how to identify and confront limiting money ideas, create a profitable money mentality, and connect your financial behaviors with your newfound beliefs in the next chapters. You will discover how to use the law of attraction to generate plenty and develop successful financial habits to help you on your path to financial well-being.

This path may need introspection, self-reflection, and, at times, a willingness to venture outside of your comfort zone. However, with each step you take toward changing your money thinking, you'll be one step closer to building a financial reality that matches your objectives and desires. Remember, everything starts with the strength of your money attitude.

Chapter 2: Uncovering Your Money Beliefs

Return to the path of changing your money mentality in "Money Mindset Makeover: Transform Your Beliefs to Attract Abundance." We're going to take a deep dive into the intriguing realm of your money ideas and attitudes in this chapter. You'll have a much better grasp of the positive and negative money attitudes that have impacted your financial thinking over the years by the conclusion of this chapter. We'll discover the unseen influences that have impacted your financial choices and create the scene for continued change via self-reflection and practical activities.

Money Subconscious Beliefs

Our connection with money is complex, complicated, and deeply rooted. It's like a tree's roots that extend under the surface and influence everything we see above ground. Our money beliefs are represented by these roots. These ideas, some of which are buried deep inside our subconscious, have a significant impact on how we manage money in our everyday lives.

Consider your money beliefs to be the glasses through which you perceive the financial world. Your perspective of money will be similarly warped if these glasses are twisted or prejudiced. Recognizing and refining these lenses may be the key to realizing your maximum financial potential.

Investigating the Belief System

Years of events, upbringing, social influences, and cultural conventions shape our money views. Some of these ideas may be powerful and beneficial to your financial objectives, while others can be restrictive and prevent you from achieving financial success. This chapter will look at how to identify and analyze these ideas, bringing them to the surface for scrutiny.

The Influence of Self-Reflection

The first step in discovering your money beliefs is self-reflection. It entails taking a step back and assessing your money-related ideas, emotions, and prior experiences. This allows you to start identifying the patterns and themes that have affected your financial choices.

Journaling is a useful self-reflection technique. Begin by devoting time to writing about your first recollections of money. Consider how money was spoken in your family, how your parents handled money, and any noteworthy financial situations that influenced you. You may learn about the roots of your money views by looking into your history.

Recognizing Positive Money Beliefs

Not all money views are harmful. Some of your beliefs, in fact, maybe powerful and serve as a solid basis for your financial well-being. Positive money attitudes may include ideas such as:

Money is a tool for creating the life I want: If you feel that money is a tool for achieving your objectives and living the life you want, you are optimistic about its possibilities.

Financial literacy is critical: The concept that continual financial education is required to make informed judgments is a powerful mentality that may lead to prudent financial decisions.

Investing in oneself yields the highest returns: If you emphasize personal growth and skill development, you will almost certainly see a return on investment in the form of greater earning potential.

Giving is receiving: A healthy attitude toward money reflects the concept that giving and charity may lead to personal affluence.

Identify these positive money concepts and appreciate their influence on your financial path throughout your self-reflection. They are useful assets in your quest for financial change.

Recognizing Money-Limiting Beliefs

Limiting attitudes, in contrast to good money views, might stymie your financial growth. These are the ideas that cloud your financial choices and limit your capacity to reach your objectives. Common money-limiting beliefs include:

Money is the source of all evil: This idea may lead to aversion to riches or self-destructive acts to escape perceived immorality linked with money.

I'll never be wealthy: Believing that financial achievement is out of reach might create a self-fulfilling cycle of financial hardship.

Moncy docs not grow on trccs, and having a scarcity mentality may lead to extreme frugality and missed investment possibilities.

Rich people are greedy: If you see prosperity as the result of greed, you may automatically ignore chances to accumulate riches.

The Influence of Money Lessons in Childhood

Our childhood is one of the most major effects on our money views. We absorb the financial lessons imparted to us by our parents, guardians, and caregivers as youngsters. These teachings, whether explicit or tacit, impact our financial outlook. If you grew up in a family where money was a cause of conflict or secrecy, you may have internalized scarcity or fear ideas.

Consider your early encounters with money to reveal these assumptions. How were your parents or guardians with money? Were they forthcoming about their financial position, or was it a taboo topic? The answers to these questions might provide information about the ideas you received and absorbed.

Common Money Belief Types

Let's group money beliefs into common topics to help you explore them:

Scarcity vs. Abundance: This topic is about whether you believe there are enough riches to go around. Wealth is seen as restricted by scarcity believers, but abundance believers perceive it as plentiful and accessible.

Growth vs. Fixed: Do you feel your financial condition may improve and develop over time, or do you believe it is set in stone and unchangeable?

Optimism vs. Pessimism: How do you see your financial future in general? Are you optimistic about your financial prospects, or are you usually pessimistic?

Courage vs. Fear: How you tackle financial difficulties and opportunities may tell a lot about your views. Do you confront them with confidence, or do you avoid them out of fear?

How do you deal with financial setbacks? Are you resilient or helpless? Do you feel resilient and motivated to recover, or do you feel powerless and defeated?

Exercises in Practice

Engage in the following practical tasks to fully understand your money ideas and attitudes:

1. The Money Timeline: Make a timeline of your financial life, beginning with your first recollections of money and progressing through key financial events to the present. Fill in the blanks with your feelings, ideas, and beliefs at each step.

2. Money Journaling: Schedule a regular time to write down your ideas and emotions concerning money. Be truthful with yourself, and investigate any emotional responses you have to financial issues.

3. Examine Your Past: If feasible, speak with family members or others who had a big role in your development and inquire about their financial ideas and attitudes. This might give further information on the origins of your money ideas.

4. Introspective Questions: Consider the following questions: What is my first recollection of money? What are my thoughts on saving, spending, and investing? What do I think about the likelihood of financial success? These questions might help you reflect on yourself.

Your Financial Beliefs: Work in Progress

It's important to remember that your money beliefs are not fixed in stone as you reveal them. While some ideas may have impacted your financial decisions for years, they are not unchangeable. You have the ability to alter and change your money beliefs so that they correspond to your financial objectives and desires.

In the next chapters, we will look at methods and tactics for challenging and changing limiting money attitudes and cultivating a thriving money mentality. Remember, recognizing your thoughts and attitudes about money is the first step toward financial change.

Chapter 3: The Limiting Money Beliefs

Welcome to the next critical step in your journey, "Money Mindset Makeover: Transform Your Beliefs to Attract Abundance." This chapter will go deeply into the area of restricting money ideas. We'll look at the most frequent money attitudes that prevent individuals from reaching financial success. Scarcity thinking, dread of achievement, and the conviction that money is the source of all evil are examples of these attitudes. Our purpose is to assist you in recognizing and confronting these negative thoughts to clear the route to abundance.

The Constraints of Money Beliefs

Consider your mind to be a garden. There are both gorgeous, blossoming flowers and dangerous weeds in this garden. Flowers symbolize your powerful and uplifting money attitudes, whilst weeds reflect your limiting money ideas. These restricting ideas often go undetected, yet if left unchecked, they have the potential to suffocate your financial success.

The first step in changing your money thinking is recognizing and confronting your limiting money beliefs. They serve as impediments to your financial success, keeping you from attaining your full potential.

Thinking about Scarcity

Scarcity thinking is one of the most typical restricting money mindsets. Scarcity thinkers are always concerned about not having enough. They feel that money is a limited resource and that every dollar spent reduces the amount of money in their bank account. This thinking creates extreme frugality and a dread of financial danger.

Confronting Scarcity Thinking: It is critical to redefine your belief in plenty to overcome scarcity thinking. Challenge the notion that there is a finite amount of money available. Recognize that money circulates and flows throughout the economy and that chances for development and success abound. By changing your viewpoint, you might discover money possibilities that you would have missed otherwise.

The Fear of Success

Fear of success, believe it or not, is a huge hurdle for many individuals. It may seem contradictory, but fear of success may be just as crippling as dread of failure. Those who are afraid of success are often concerned about the duties and expectations that come with it. They may even be concerned that their success would cause them to be estranged from loved ones or result in a loss of personal independence.

Confronting Your Fear of Success: Confronting your fear of success requires a thorough grasp of your unique beliefs and objectives. What is it that you cherish in life? What are your fundamental ideas about success and its consequences? You may overcome your fear of success by establishing your values and defining success on your terms. Remember that success does not have to imply a loss of liberty or estrangement from loved ones. You can determine your definition of success.

The source of all evil is money.

Many civilizations have the concept that money is the source of all evil. It is based on the idea that pursuing riches might lead to immoral actions and moral degeneration. This notion might inhibit individuals from aggressively achieving financial success because they are afraid of the negative repercussions.

Taking on the "Money is Evil" Belief: To refute the notion that money is intrinsically bad, it is necessary to distinguish between the desire for riches and immoral action. Money is inherently neutral; it is up to people's decisions and actions to decide whether it is utilized for good or bad. Accept the notion that money can be a constructive force for change and that financial success may allow you to make a difference in your own life and the lives of others.

The Narratives We Create for Ourselves

It's critical to realize the tales you've been telling yourself as you address these limiting money ideas. We all have personal money stories that impact our behavior and choices. These tales can either reinforce or encourage you to reach financial plenty.

The Victim's Account

Some people consider themselves as victims of their financial situation. They may attribute their financial difficulties to external causes such as the economy, their upbringing, or a lack of chances. This victim attitude keeps them trapped in a cycle of financial difficulty.

Confronting the Victim's Tale: It is critical to accept responsibility for your financial condition to confront the victim's tale. Recognize that, although external conditions might be difficult, you have the ability to make decisions and take actions that affect your financial destiny. Give yourself the ability to make proactive financial choices.

The Scarcity Narrative

Scarcity thinking is strongly tied to the scarcity tale. Individuals in this story feel that no matter how hard they work, they will never have enough money. They are continuously concerned about running out of money and living in terror of financial insecurity.

Overcoming the Scarcity tale: Overcoming the scarcity tale requires a mental adjustment. Begin by admitting that you have the potential to generate financial stability. Concentrate on the concrete measures you can take to create a financial safety net and prepare for the future. You may replace the scarcity tale with one of wealth and security by taking charge of your money.

The Story of Self-Worth

Many individuals associate their self-worth with financial achievement. If they are suffering financially, they may feel unworthy or inadequate. This might result in emotions of embarrassment and self-doubt.

Confronting the Self-Worth Story: It is critical to keep your self-worth independent from your financial status. Your money balance does not define your worth as a person. Recognize that your sense of self-worth is inherent and unrelated to your financial achievement. You may seek financial success without being tormented by self-doubt if you have a good sense of self-worth.

Exercises in Practice

Engage in the following practical tasks to face and overcome your limiting money beliefs:

1. Belief Analysis: Make two columns on a sheet of paper. List your money-limiting beliefs in the left column. In the right column, provide evidence to refute each belief. For example, if your limiting belief is "I'll never have enough money," confront it with examples of occasions when you did have enough money for your requirements.

2. Positive Affirmations: Create affirmations that contradict your limiting thoughts. For example, if you struggle with the concept that money is bad, write an affirmation that says, "Money is a tool for creating positive change in my life and the lives of others." Repeat these affirmations every day to help your new beliefs stick.

3. Visualization: Close your eyes and see yourself in the future, having conquered your limiting money beliefs and achieving financial prosperity. Visualize the particular results you want. This exercise might assist you in shifting your mentality from scarcity to abundance.

4. Education: Learn about personal money, wealth-building tactics, and personal financial success stories. Learning how others overcame limiting attitudes and accomplished their financial objectives may inspire and drive you.

Conclusion

Confronting and questioning your limiting money ideas is a transforming process that opens the door to wealth. You're taking a huge step toward financial independence and satisfaction by identifying the influence of scarcity thinking, the fear of success, and the assumption that money is the source of all evil. As you continue on your quest, keep in mind that these deeply embedded ideas are not insurmountable. You may replace these limiting ideas with powerful ones that coincide with your financial goals with commitment, self-awareness, and the correct tools. The bravery to confront your money anxieties and break free from the shackles of limiting ideas is the first step on the road to plenty.

Chapter 4: Cultivating a Prosperous Money Mindset

Welcome to the life-changing experience that is "Money Mindset Makeover: Transform Your Beliefs to Attract Abundance." After delving into the realm of limiting money attitudes in the last chapter, it's time to flip the page and start creating a flourishing money mentality. In this chapter, we'll provide you with a toolbox of tactics for replacing limiting ideas with empowering ones, adopting a growth mindset, and setting good financial aspirations. It's a path toward a mentality that not only attracts plenty but also enables you to maximize it.

Paradigm Shift: From Scarcity to Abundance

Your money attitude, as we've learned, is a tremendous force that molds your financial reality. Money ideas that are too restrictive might function as anchors, keeping you from sailing toward the beaches of financial wealth. To break free from these shackles and set sail on a wealthy adventure, you must create a prosperous money attitude. But what exactly does it mean?

A successful money attitude is not about amassing wealth to accumulate riches. Instead, it is a mindset that embraces and capitalizes on chances for growth, prosperity, and personal development. It's a way of thinking that believes in the prospect of plenty and sees money as a tool for attaining personal and social objectives.

Changing Limiting Beliefs for Empowering Beliefs

The first step in developing a productive money mentality is to recognize limiting ideas and replace them with powerful ones. This is a process of retraining your subconscious mind and rewriting the stories that have kept you stuck. Here's how to go about it:

1. Become aware of the limiting thoughts that have been working in your life. These might include beliefs such as "I'll never be wealthy" or

"Money is the root of all evil." The first step toward transformation is recognizing them.

2. Challenge: After you've discovered your limiting beliefs, put them to the test. Consider if your opinions are founded on facts or are only assumptions. Seek evidence that contradicts these ideas. If you believe that "money is the root of all evil," think about how money may also be utilized for charity and good transformation.

3. Rewrite the story: Begin rewriting the story with your increased knowledge and challenges to your limiting beliefs. Replace these beliefs with statements that empower you. Change "I'll never be wealthy" to "I am capable of building wealth over time." The key to making these affirmations particular, positive, and present tense is to make them specific, positive, and present tense.

4. Repetition: It is critical to retrain your mind by repeating your powerful ideas. The more you reinforce your new ideas, the more they will become ingrained in your cognitive processes. Consider making daily affirmations to strengthen your positive thoughts.

5. Visualize: Visualization is a very effective method. Imagine yourself living the life you want and achieving the financial success you want. Visualization not only reinforces your new views but also increases your drive to act.

Developing a Growth Mindset

A profitable money mentality is inextricably linked to the idea of a development mindset. A growth mindset, as defined by psychologist Carol Dweck, is the concept that talents and intellect can be improved through devotion and hard effort. This perspective is the polar opposite of a fixed mindset, which holds that talents are innate and immutable.

When it comes to your money, adopting a growth mindset implies thinking that you can increase your financial knowledge, make better judgments, and eventually attain financial success via hard work and study. Here are some tips for cultivating a development mentality in your financial life:

1. Accept Challenges: Rather than avoiding financial difficulties, embrace them as chances for progress. When faced with a financial dilemma or choice, see it as an opportunity to learn and grow.

2. Constant Learning: Commit to continued financial education. Invest in your financial education by reading books, taking classes, or obtaining guidance from professionals. The more you learn, the more prepared you will be to make sound judgments.

3. Effort Is Important: Recognize the importance of work in financial success. It's not merely a matter of natural aptitude or good fortune. The time and effort you put into managing your money and seeking out possibilities may make a big impact.

4. View setbacks as opportunities for learning: Setbacks are unavoidable in the quest for financial achievement. Rather than seeing them as failures, consider them chances to learn, adapt, and develop.

5. Feedback Is Important: Financial mentors or advisers are welcome to provide input. Constructive comments might give insights that will allow you to make better choices and make changes to your financial goals.

Making Good Financial Decisions

Your attitudes and beliefs might influence your financial decisions. Setting good financial intentions allows you to connect your mentality with your money objectives. Intentions serve as a road map for your activities and choices. Here's how to make good financial decisions:

1. identify Your Financial Objectives: Identify your financial objectives. Do you want to attain financial independence, purchase a house, establish a company, or contribute to a cause that is important to you? Your objectives must be explicit and quantifiable.

2. Align with Your Values: Make sure your financial objectives are in line with your values and ideals. When your objectives are aligned with what is most important to you, you are more likely to remain motivated.

3. Break Down Your Objectives: Break down your financial objectives into smaller, more attainable stages. This makes things less intimidating and more attainable. It also lets you keep track of your progress.

Create affirmations that represent your optimistic financial aspirations. If your objective is to save money, for example, your affirmation may be, "I am committed to saving [specific amount] every month."

5. Visualize Success: Imagine yourself reaching your financial objectives. Consider your emotions, your feeling of achievement, and your lifestyle. This vision may both encourage and inspire you to act.

Exercises in Practice

Consider the following activities to help you create a wealthy money mindset:

1. regular Affirmations: Write down and say inspiring affirmations relating to your financial objectives regularly. Here's an example: "I am on the path to financial success, and I embrace every opportunity to learn and grow."

2. Create a financial vision board to graphically depict your financial objectives. Include pictures, phrases, and symbols that motivate you and serve as reminders of your goals.

3. Growth diary: Keep a diary in which you document your financial journey, including problems, accomplishments, and lessons gained. Consider how you've adopted a development attitude.

4. Accountability Partner: Enlist the help of a trustworthy friend or mentor who can keep you responsible for your financial goals. Share your objectives and progress with them frequently.

Conclusion

Cultivating a thriving money attitude is a transforming and powerful experience. You're laying the groundwork for financial prosperity and success by replacing limiting ideas with empowering ones, adopting a growth mindset, and making good financial objectives.

Your attitude is the compass that directs your financial choices, and with the appropriate compass, you can confidently and purposefully traverse the difficult landscape of personal finance. Remember that it's not just about the goal as you continue your trip; it's about the development, learning, and empowerment you encounter along the way.

Chapter 5: The Law of Attraction and Money

This is Chapter 5 of the book "Money Mindset Makeover: Transform Your Beliefs to Attract Abundance." In this chapter, we'll delve into the fascinating realm of the law of attraction and its deep relationship with money. We'll look at the complex link between your money ideas, emotions, and beliefs and their impact on attracting or rejecting financial chances. By the conclusion of this chapter, you will not only grasp the concepts of the law of attraction, but you will also know how to use it to materialize the prosperity and plenty you want.

The Secret of the Law of Attraction

The law of attraction has received a lot of attention in recent years, owing in part to publications like "The Secret" by Rhonda Byrne. But what is the law of attraction precisely, and how does it relate to money and financial success?

The law of attraction is a universal concept that states that similar things attract like things. In other words, the energy you release via your thoughts and emotions attracts energy from the cosmos that is comparable to it. This may have both good and bad forms. Focusing on good thoughts and emotions increases your chances of attracting pleasant experiences and opportunities, even financial ones. Negative thinking, on the other hand, might attract unfavorable conditions and financial challenges.

The Power of Your Thoughts and the Law of Attraction

Your ideas heavily influenced the law of attraction. The energy you produce with your ideas is similar to a magnetic force that attracts events and possibilities into your life. When it comes to money, your ideas may work as a magnet or a repellant to financial success.

Consider this: If you are continually concerned about not having enough money, your thoughts are vibrating at a lack and scarcity frequency.

The law of attraction reacts by bringing you additional circumstances that match those vibrations, prolonging your financial difficulties. However, focusing your mind on the abundance you seek sends forth vibrations of money and prosperity, which might attract financial chances and success.

The Importance of Feelings and Emotions

While ideas are powerful, emotions are what drive the law of attraction. Emotions act like rocket fuel, propelling your aspirations into the cosmos. When you are sincerely enthusiastic about your financial objectives, you create a strong magnetic field that attracts opportunities and resources to you.

If you have worry, anxiety, or concern about money, you are putting out vibrations that repel the same wealth you need. Aligning your thoughts and emotions is critical for establishing a harmonic resonance that attracts your financial aspirations.

The Subconscious Mind and Beliefs

Your beliefs, particularly those held subconsciously, are critical to the law of attraction. While you may want financial success and wealth consciously, your subconscious beliefs may either support or oppose those aspirations. For example, if you consciously want riches but subconsciously believe that it is immoral or unachievable, your subconscious beliefs will take precedence over your conscious goals.

To fully use the law of attraction, you must link your subconscious beliefs with your conscious objectives. This entails recognizing, confronting, and replacing any limiting money beliefs with powerful ones.

Using the Law of Attraction to Align Your Money Mindset

Consider the following concepts and tactics to connect your money thinking with the law of attraction:

1. identify Your Financial Ambitions and Desires: Identify your financial ambitions and desires. Be explicit about the money and prosperity you want.

2. Visualization: Visualize yourself living the life you want with financial success regularly. Consider the particulars of this existence, including emotions of satisfaction and delight.

3. Affirmations: Make affirmations that represent your financial objectives and your confidence in their achievement. Affirm these phrases oftentimes to strengthen your optimistic thinking.

4. Thanks: Express thanks for the prosperity and richness you currently have. Developing a grateful attitude improves your vibrational frequency and attracts more of what you value.

5. Let Go of Negative Feelings: Work on letting go of any negative feelings or thoughts you have regarding money. Techniques such as meditation, mindfulness, or therapy may be used to treat prior traumas or negative conditioning.

6. Surround Yourself with Positivity: Surround yourself with individuals who support your financial objectives and have a good attitude. Your social circle's energy may have a major influence on your energy and views.

7. Take Inspired Action: The law of attraction does not need you to sit around and wait for money to appear. It is about taking motivated, deliberate activities toward your financial objectives. When your ideas and emotions are in sync with your actions, you create a tremendous magnet for success.

Techniques for Applying the Law of Attraction

Here are some methods for using the law of attraction to your financial goals:

1. Create a vision board that graphically communicates your financial goals. Include pictures, phrases, and symbols that are relevant

to your objectives. Put it somewhere, and you'll see it every day.

2. Meditation: Practicing meditation regularly might help you connect your thoughts and emotions with your financial goals. Visualize and experience the feelings linked with financial achievement during meditation.

3. Journaling: Keep a diary in which you write about your financial objectives, progress, and pleasant money experiences. This technique strengthens your emphasis on plenty.

4. Affirmation Cards: Make affirmation cards with inspiring money and wealth phrases. Carry them about with you and go over them throughout the day.

5. Act as If: Model your actions and thinking after someone who has already attained the financial success you want. This might assist you in shifting your vibration to one of plenty.

Stories of Success

The law of attraction has been a motivating element behind many personal financial success stories. Numerous people have improved their financial lives by using the power of their ideas, emotions, and beliefs. These tales serve as motivating examples of what is achievable when your money thinking is in sync with the law of attraction.

The Success of the Entrepreneur

Consider a prospective entrepreneur who, although having a fantastic company concept, lacks the financial wherewithal to put it into action. Frustrated by a lack of funding, the entrepreneur decided to use the principles of the law of attraction. They started to see their company growing, drawing customers, and earning big cash. They rehearsed affirmations of financial prosperity every morning and had a clear picture of their company's success.

Within months, a succession of unexpected chances presented themselves. They were approached by an angel investor who believed in their concept and gave the required funds. The company went off, outperforming even its most optimistic predictions. The entrepreneur had used the law of attraction to bring about financial success.

The Road to Financial Freedom

Another person found themselves trapped behind a pile of debt, unable to make ends meet. They started to apply the concepts of the law of attraction to their financial predicament. Instead of focusing on the debt, they concentrated on emotions of financial independence and prosperity. They practiced being grateful for the resources they did have and imagined being debt-free.

Over time, the person began to receive unexpected windfalls, such as a job bonus and money presents from family members.

Chapter 6: Financial Habits and Abundance

The following is Chapter 6 of "Money Mindset Makeover: Transform Your Beliefs to Attract Abundance." In this chapter, we'll go from attitude to actual use of your newfound financial empowerment. Building a solid money attitude is essential, but it is your everyday financial habits and actions that will convert your dreams into reality. We'll talk about how successful budgeting, saving, and investing tactics that line with your money attitude may help you achieve long-term financial plenty.

The Critical Relationship Between Habits and Abundance

Your thinking is the captain of the ship, guiding your financial route. However, the crew that executes those commands is made up of your everyday financial behaviors. These are the activities, behaviors, and choices that you repeat regularly. They either support or oppose your financial objectives.

To materialize financial prosperity, you must first acknowledge the impact of your behaviors. Abundance does not arise by coincidence; it is the product of deliberate decisions and disciplined activities. Let's look at five critical financial practices that may help you get there.

Budgeting Effectively: Your Financial Navigation System

A budget is like a financial GPS. It serves as a road map for your spending and saving choices. Without a budget, your financial path lacks direction and is easy to deviate from. It is critical to create and adhere to an appropriate budget to attain long-term abundance.

Setting Up Your Budget Income: Begin by noting your sources of income, such as your salary, any side hustle profits, rental income, or investment dividends. Be thorough and precise.

Expenses: Next, list your monthly expenditures. Rent or mortgage, utilities, food, transit costs, insurance, debt repayments, entertainment, and other expenses may be included. Don't forget to budget for one-time or yearly costs such as vacations or auto maintenance.

Distinguish desires from requirements: Examine your costs and distinguish between desires and requirements. Needs are necessities for your fundamental well-being, such as shelter and food, while desires are non-essential purchases or experiences.

Prioritize Savings: Make savings a priority in your budget. Contributions to retirement accounts, emergency reserves, and investment accounts are examples of this.

Set Financial Objectives: Allocate a percentage of your budget to specific financial objectives, such as debt repayment, house savings, or school investments.

Maintaining Your Budget

Once you've created your budget, it's critical to monitor your actual spending against it. This allows you to discover areas where you may be overspending and make changes to remain on track.

There are several tools and applications available to help budgeting and monitoring your expenditures easier. Consider using these tools to keep your finances organized and accessible.

Making Budget Changes

A budget is not a fixed document. Life is fluid, and your financial situation may change. It is critical to analyze and alter your budget frequently. For example, if your pay increases, you may decide to put extra money aside for savings or investing. In contrast, if you incur unanticipated costs, you may need to lower your spending in other areas.

By evaluating and updating your budget regularly, you ensure that it continues to represent your financial objectives and goals.

The Influence of Saving

One of the essential financial practices that might lead to affluence is saving. It provides protection and peace of mind by acting as a financial safety net. Saving may also serve as a springboard for future wealth creation and investment possibilities.

Emergency Reserve Fund

An emergency fund is an essential part of any savings strategy. It is a financial reserve put up to handle unexpected costs such as medical bills, auto repairs, or job loss. When unexpected financial issues happen, an emergency fund guarantees that you do not have to depend on credit cards or loans.

Financial gurus often advise keeping three to six months' worth of living costs in your emergency fund. The appropriate amount, however, will depend on your own circumstances and risk tolerance.

Accounts for Savings

Consider utilizing high-yield savings accounts or certificates of deposit (CDs) for short- and medium-term objectives. These accounts provide higher interest rates than regular savings accounts. They give a secure location for your money while collecting interest.

Retirement Funds

Retirement savings is a long-term financial objective that should be prioritized. Contributing to retirement plans such as a 401(k) or IRA may provide considerable tax benefits while also assisting you in building wealth for the future.

Because of the power of compound interest, early and regular contributions to your retirement funds are critical. The more you save and the sooner you begin, the longer your investments have to grow.

Investing for Prosperity

Investing is an important financial habit that may help you transition from saving to affluence. While saving maintains your money, investing has the potential to considerably increase it. It does, however, come with hazards that must be controlled.

Various Investments

There are several investing choices available, including:

Stocks: Owning a company's stock allows you to a piece of its earnings and losses. Stocks offer the potential for large profits, but they also carry a greater degree of risk and volatility.

Bonds are loans made to governments or enterprises. They are deemed less risky than equities but provide lesser rewards.

Real estate investing may be profitable due to property appreciation and rental revenue.

Mutual funds aggregate money from different individuals to invest in a diverse portfolio of stocks, bonds, and other assets.

ETFs: ETFs are comparable to mutual funds, except they trade on stock exchanges like individual equities.

Retirement plans, such as 401(k)s and IRAs, provide tax benefits for long-term investment.

Diversification

Diversification is an important risk-management approach in your investing portfolio. It entails diversifying your assets among asset classes, sectors, and geographic locations. You may decrease the effect of a single investment's bad performance on your whole portfolio by diversifying.

Long-Term Prospects

Investing for plenty requires a long-term mindset. The stock market, for example, may be turbulent in the near term, but it has traditionally exhibited stable growth over long periods of time. It is critical that you can weather market volatility while remaining loyal to your financial plan.

Tolerance for Risk

Your risk tolerance is an important consideration when developing an investing plan. It is critical to match your risk tolerance with your investing strategy. If you are risk-averse, you may choose more cautious investments, whilst others with a greater risk tolerance may prefer more aggressive investments.

Chapter 7: Sustaining Your Money Mindset Makeover

Congratulations on finishing "Money Mindset Makeover: Transform Your Beliefs to Attract Abundance." You've been on a journey of self-discovery and development, from identifying your limiting money beliefs to establishing a flourishing money attitude. In this last chapter, we'll go over the measures you need to take to guarantee that your money attitude revolution isn't just a fad. We'll show you how to keep your newfound beliefs, stick to your financial objectives, and keep attracting wealth into your life.

The Difficulty of Maintaining Change

As you've seen during this trip, changing your money perspective is a continuous process rather than a one-time event. While you have made tremendous progress in changing your beliefs and practices, the problem now is to maintain these improvements over time. Life is dynamic, and you will face a variety of external pressures, setbacks, and obstacles that will put your dedication to your new money philosophy to the test.

Maintaining your money mentality transformation involves perseverance, effort, and a proactive approach. Let's look at some techniques to assist you in keeping on track and continuing to draw wealth into your life.

Sustaining Your Money Mindset Transformation

1. Consistent Self-Reflection

Self-reflection is a continuous exercise that may assist you in staying conscious of your money perspective. Schedule frequent check-ins with yourself to examine your money assumptions and attitudes. Pose queries such as:

Do my financial choices reflect my new money mindset?

Have I reverted to old, restricting beliefs?

How far have I gotten toward my financial objectives?

You may address any negative habits or attitudes that may reappear and reaffirm your dedication to your flourishing money mentality by self-reflecting regularly.

2. Lifelong Learning

Maintaining your money attitude makeover requires being knowledgeable about personal finance and wealth-building tactics. Financial environments shift, bringing with them new possibilities and problems. Continue your education by reading books, attending seminars, and keeping current on financial news. This information enables you to make educated judgments and adjust to changing conditions.

3. Partners in Accountability

Accountability partners might help you maintain your new money perspective. These are people who share your desire for financial success and can keep you accountable for your actions and choices. You're more likely to remain on track and motivated if you routinely share your financial objectives and progress with an accountability partner.

4. Affirmation and Visualization Maintenance

Don't underestimate the power of positive affirmations and imagery. Continue to use these strategies to strengthen your wealthy money mentality. Visualize your financial objectives regularly, and repeat affirmations that reflect your thoughts and aspirations. The more you exercise certain behaviors, the more established they become in your subconscious.

5. Mistakes as Learning Experiences Setbacks and hardships are unavoidable on any path, including your money attitude transformation. Instead of perceiving setbacks as failures, consider them potential learning opportunities. Analyze what went wrong, what you can do better, and how your actions can be more in line with your ideals. Setbacks may be used as stepping stones to future achievement.

6. Avoiding Outside Influences

External factors, such as commercial messaging, cultural pressures, and other people's views, might jeopardize your money mentality transformation. It's important to be aware of these influences and shield your mind from their bad effects. Be picky about the stuff you watch and the people you interact with. Surround yourself with people who share your financial objectives and ideals.

7. Financial Goals and Objectives

Maintain a detailed financial plan with precise milestones and objectives. As your circumstances change and your aspirations expand, your strategy should develop. A well-defined financial plan serves as a road map and serves to keep you motivated. When you hit milestones, celebrate your accomplishments because it reaffirms your dedication to your money mentality transformation.

8. Conscious Spending

It is critical to practice mindful spending as you go on your path. This entails being aware of your financial decisions and how they relate to your money thinking. Avoid impulsive or emotional spending, and make choices that align with your financial objectives and values.

Embracing Abundance as a Way of Life

Maintaining your money mentality makeover is more than simply holding onto a set of ideas; it's about embracing plenty as a way of life. Abundance is an attitude of abundance, well-being, and thankfulness for all elements of life, not simply money.

Appreciation Practice: Continue to develop an appreciation for the riches in your life. Gratitude is an extremely strong positive feeling that attracts more of what you value.

Pay It Forward: When plenty is shared, it increases. Find ways to give back to your community, support organizations you care about, and assist others in reaching their financial objectives. When you help the well-being of others, you start a circle of plenty.

Take in the scenery: Remember that changing your money perspective is a lifetime process, not a destination. Accept the process, the progress, and the empowerment that it brings. Discover pleasure and contentment in your everyday financial decisions.

Adaptability and Flexibility: Be adaptable in your approach. Life is unpredictable, and things change. Adapt your techniques, objectives, and beliefs as needed, while remaining loyal to your basic financial empowerment and abundance ideas.

Summary: A Lifetime Adventure

Your money attitude transformation is a lifetime endeavor that involves dedication and self-awareness. The metamorphosis you've experienced over the last seven chapters is not an ending, but rather a fresh beginning. You are well-equipped to handle your financial path with confidence and attract continual wealth into your life if you have a profitable money attitude and the skills to maintain it.

Remember that the power of your beliefs, ideas, and deeds is a force for good change as you continue on your road. Your relationship with money is a dynamic and developing component of your life, and you have the capacity to build the prosperous and joyful life you wish by intentionally influencing it.